Read	Trace	Write
a egy		
I én		
am am		
an egy		
as mint		
at nál nél		

Read and write the sentence!

a	This is a bird.
I	I will play with the toys.
am	I am crawling on the ground.
an	This is an ant.
as	It is as light as a feather.
at	She is at her friend's house.

Read	Trace	Write
be lenni		
by által		
do csinál		
go megy		
he ő		
if ha		

Read and write the sentence!

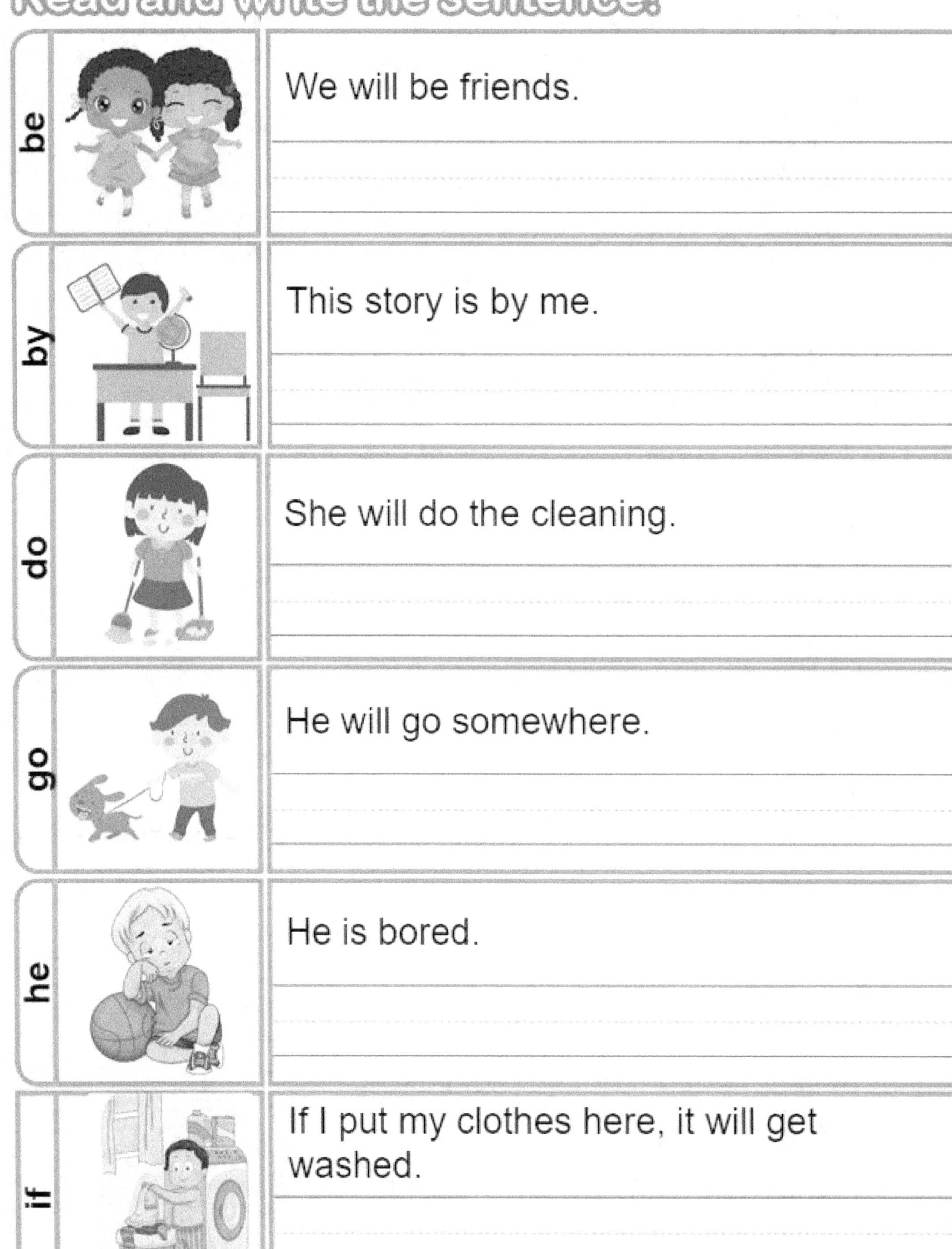

Read	Trace	Write
in ban ben		
is jelentése		
it azt		
me nekem		
my az én		
no nem		

Read and write the sentence!

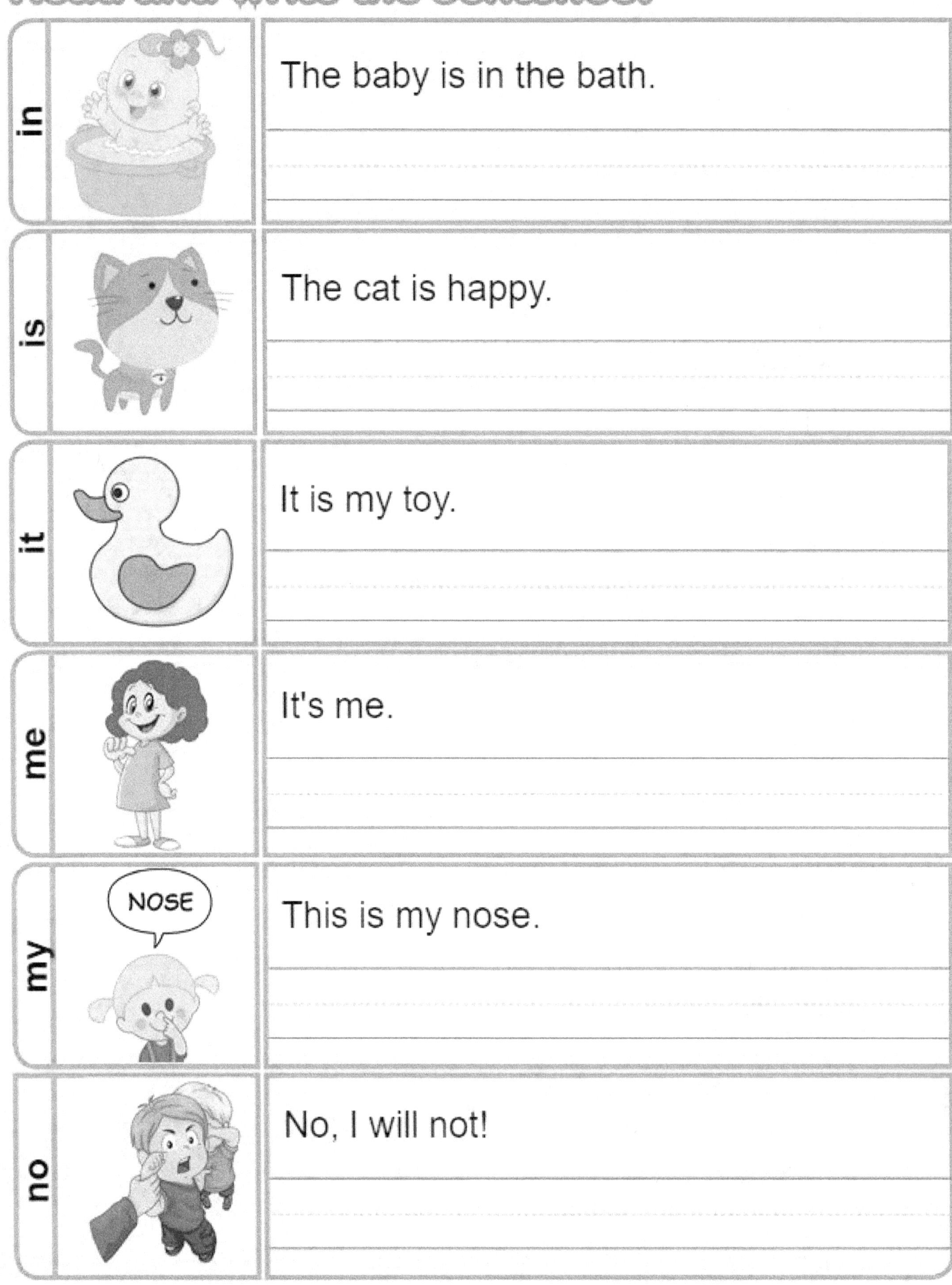

Read
Trace
Write
of
nak,-nek
on
tovább
or
vagy
so
így
to
nak nek
up
fel

Read and write the sentence!

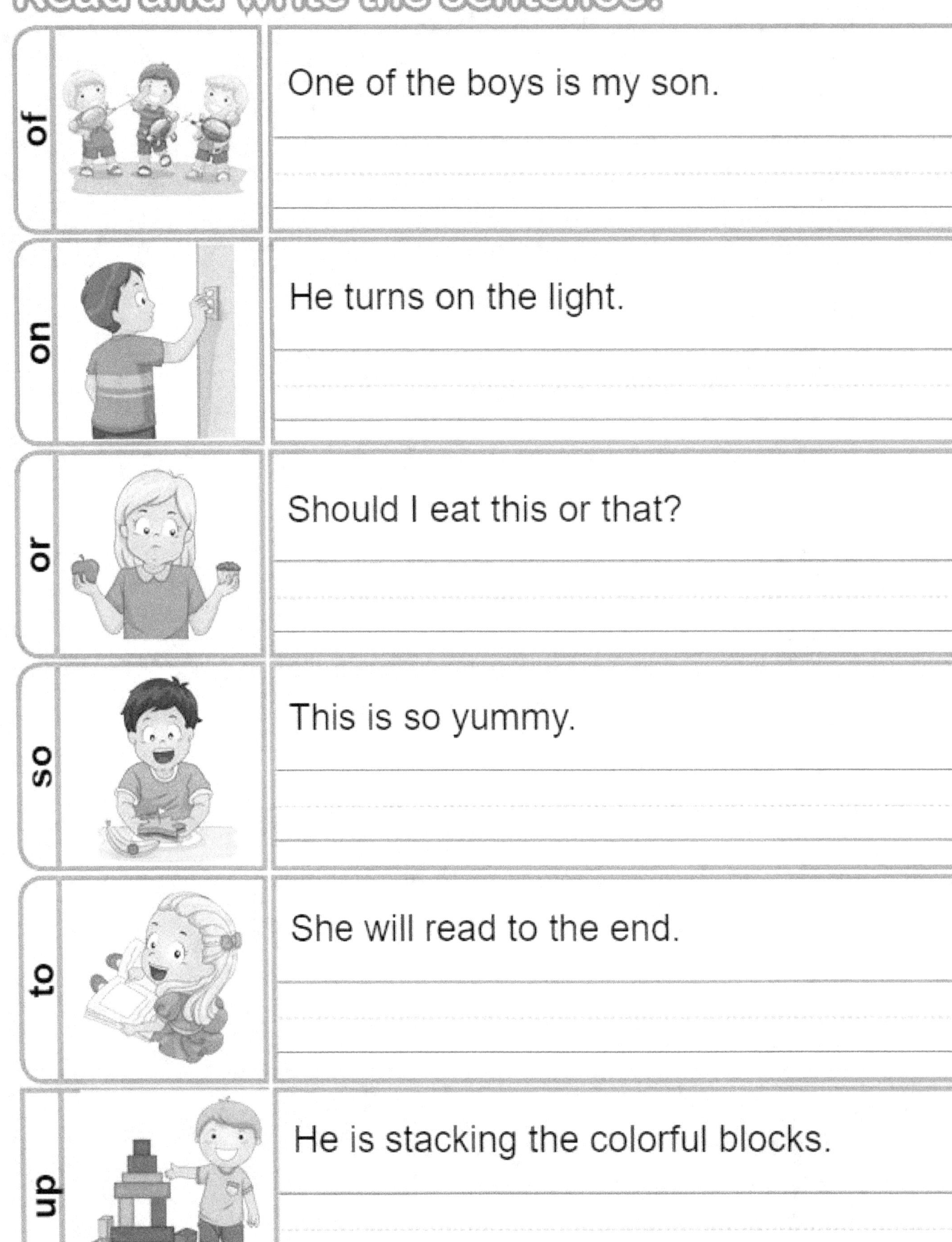

Read	Trace	Write
us minket		
we mi		
all minden		
and és		
any bármi		
are vannak		

Read and write the sentence!

us		Both of us are walking.
we		We are helping to make a house.
all		We are all dancing together.
and		My brother and I are playing.
any		They can read any books.
are		The eggs are colorful.

Read
Trace
Write
ask
kérdez
ate
evett
bed
ágy
big
nagy
box
doboz
boy
fiú

Read and write the sentence!

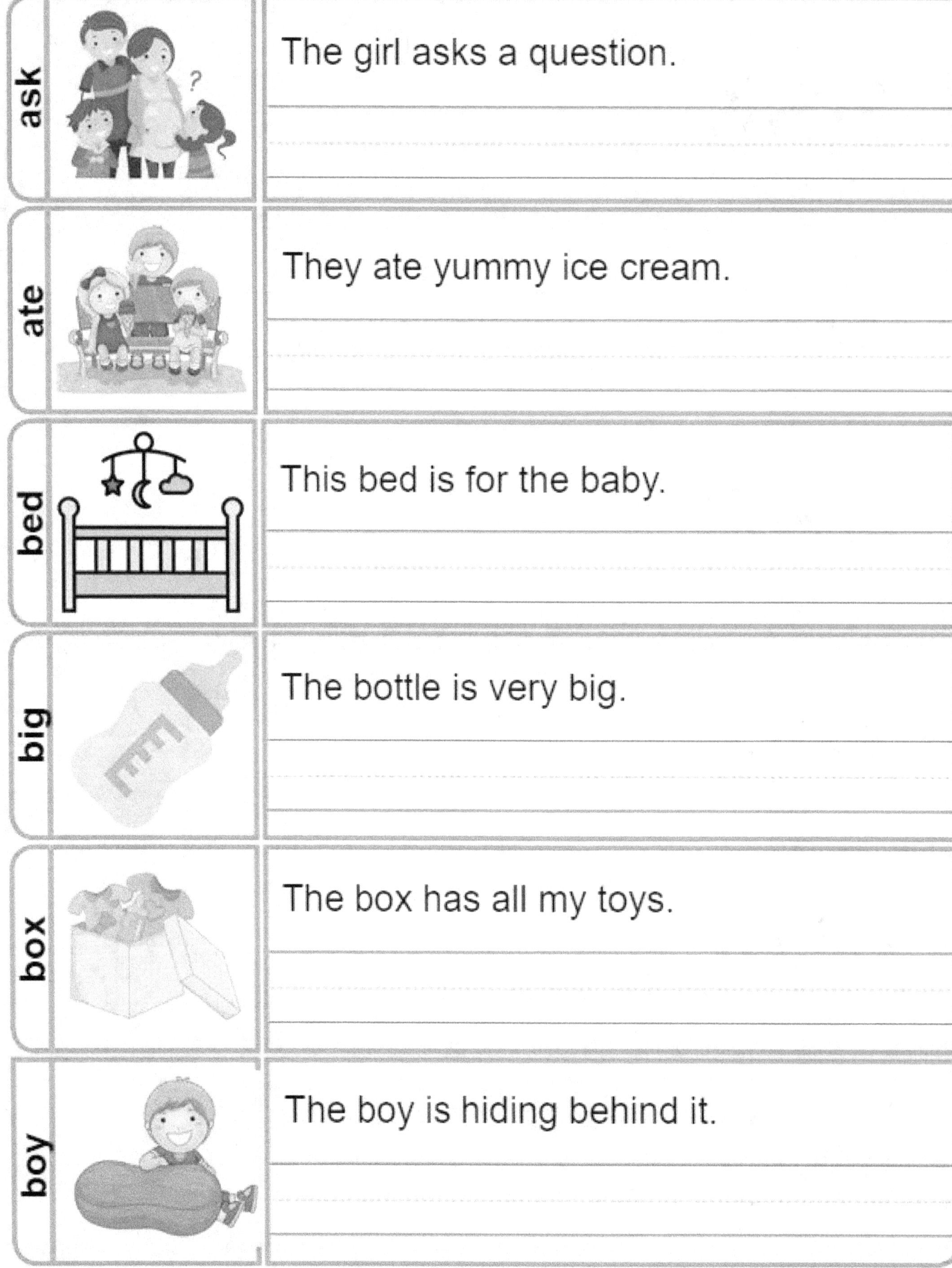

Read
Trace
Write
but
de
buy
megvesz
can
tud
car
autó
cat
macska
cow
tehén

Read and write the sentence!

but	 I want to go, but my son doesn't.
buy	 He buys lots of stuff.
can	 The baby will drink milk from the can.
car	 The car is red.
cat	 The cat is sad.
cow	 The cow is funny.

Read	Trace	Write
cut vágott		
day nap		
did tett		
dog kutya		
eat eszik		
egg tojás		

Read and write the sentence!

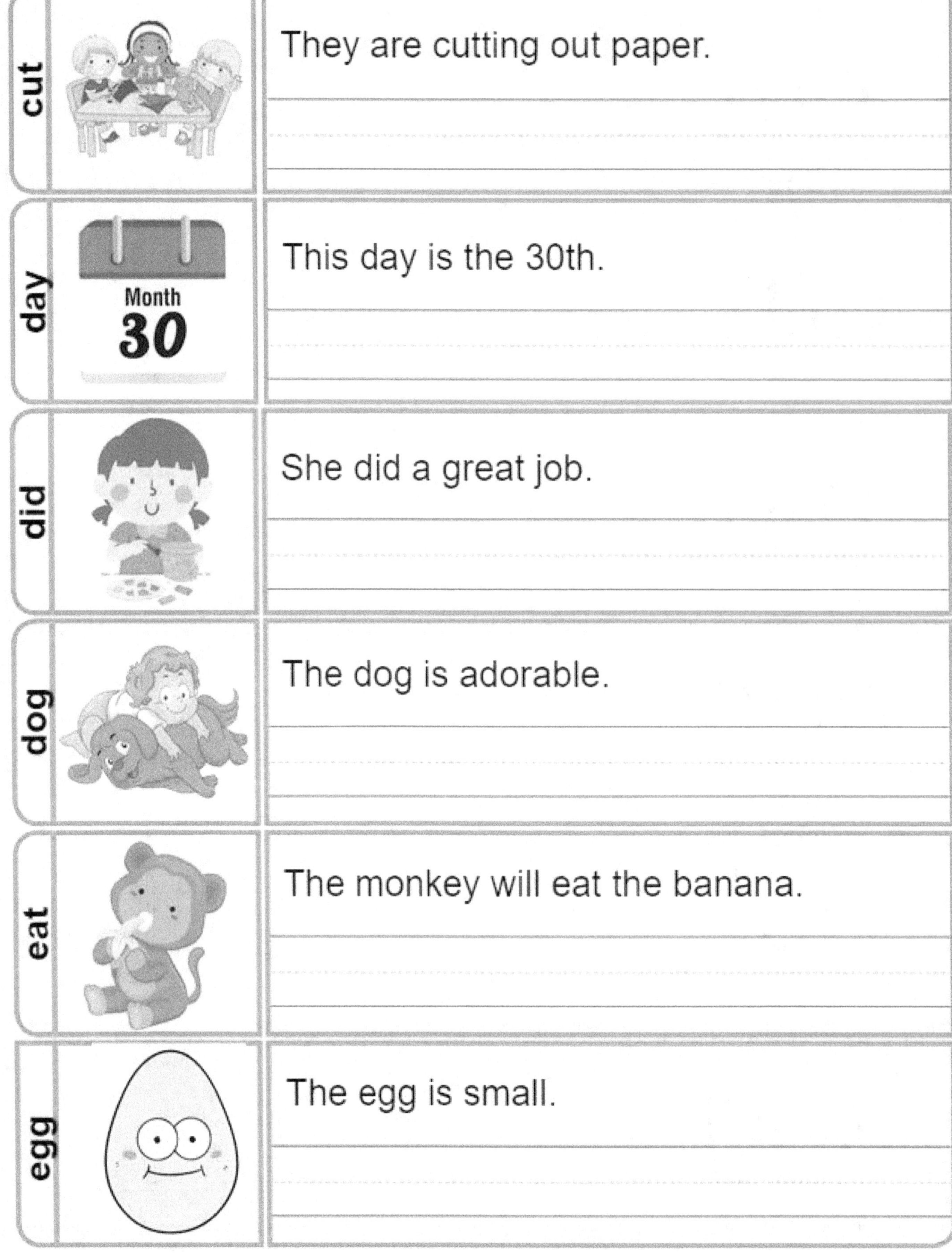

Read	Trace	Write
eye szem		
far messze		
fly légy		
for mert		
get kap		
got kapott		

Read and write the sentence!

Read
Trace
Write
had
volt
has
van
her
neki
him
neki
his
övé
hot
forró

Read and write the sentence!

Read
Trace
Write
how
hogyan
its
annak
leg
láb
let
enged
man
férfi
may
lehet

Read and write the sentence!

how	How many blocks are there?
its	Its legs are short.
leg	His legs are short.
let	Let me come in!
man	The man is a vet.
may	May I have more?

Read
Trace
Write
men
férfiak
new
új
not
nem
now
most
off
ki
old
régi

Read and write the sentence!

men	The men are mining for gold.
new	She has a new hat.
not	She is not feeling well.
now	Now I am doing my homework.
off	They cut off the paper.
old	You are one year old!

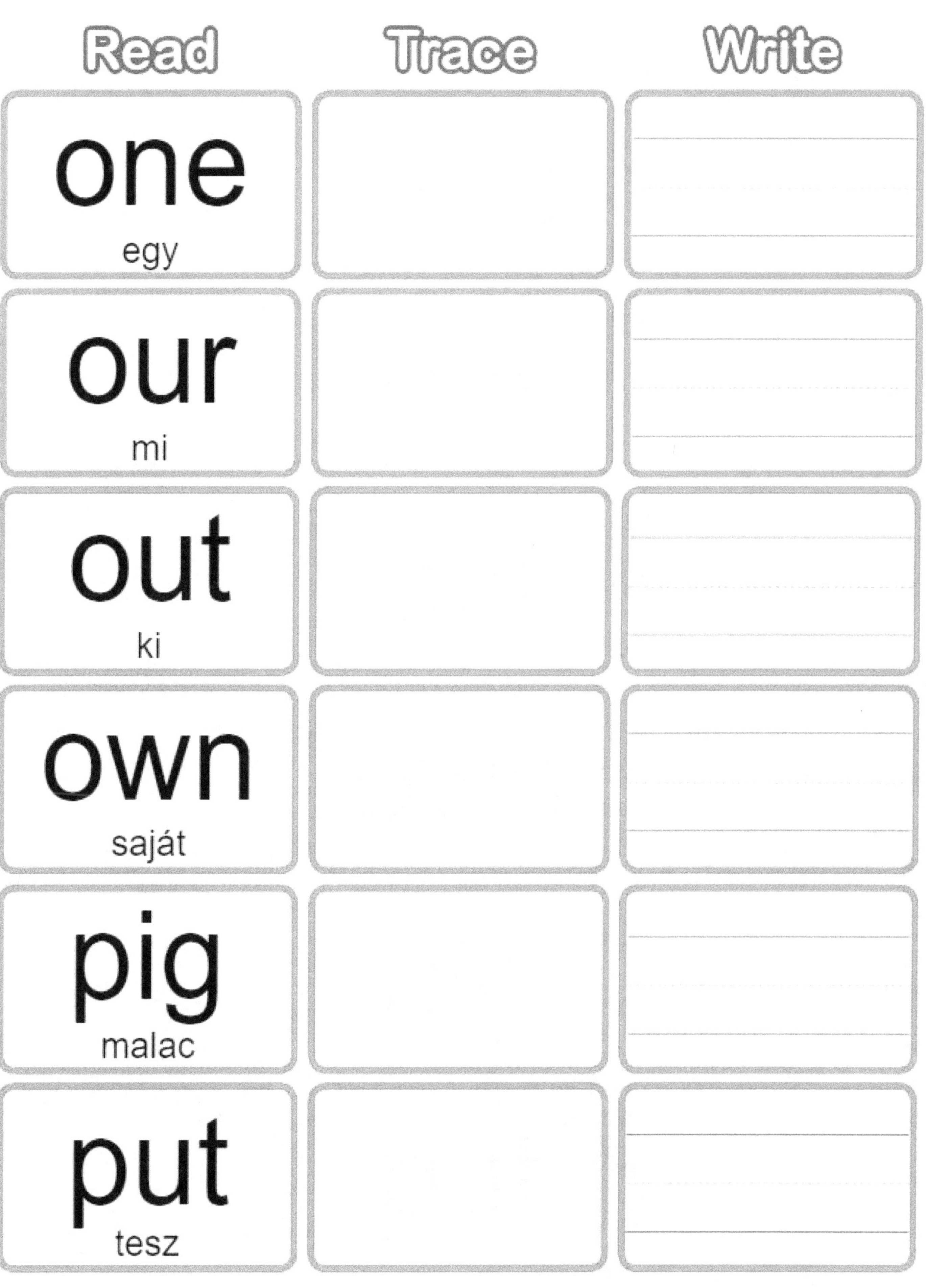

Read
Trace
Write

one
egy

our
mi

out
ki

own
saját

pig
malac

put
tesz

Read and write the sentence!

one	The panda says one.
our	This is our room.
out	He will go out.
own	The man owns a computer.
pig	She is sleeping on her pig.
put	She is putting an arm around her daughter.

Read
Trace
Write
ran
fuss
red
piros
run
fuss
saw
lát
say
mond
see
lát

Read and write the sentence!

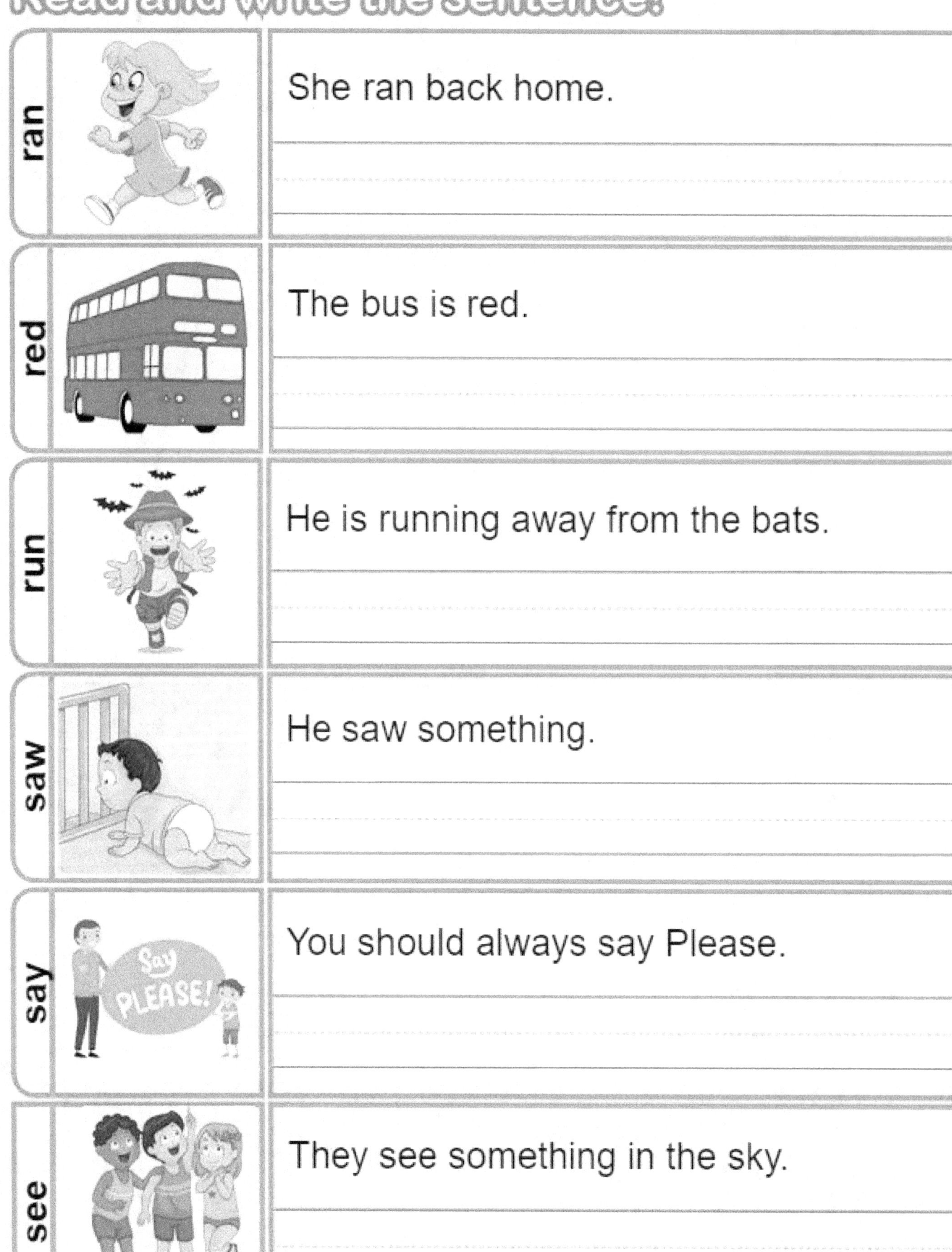

ran		She ran back home.
red		The bus is red.
run		He is running away from the bats.
saw		He saw something.
say		You should always say Please.
see		They see something in the sky.

Read
Trace
Write
she
ő
sit
ül
six
hat
sun
nap
ten
tíz
the
egy

she — She is smiling.

sit — The baby is sitting.

six — Number six is my lucky number.

sun — The sun is shining.

ten — The monkey can count to ten.

the — The baby is playing with the ball.

Read   Trace   Write

Read and write the sentence!

too	The bear is too cute.
top	The pot is on the top.
toy	The baby has lots of toys.
try	We try to be kind to him.
two	Today you have turned two.
use	I use my toothpaste and toothbrush.

Read	Trace	Write
was volt		
way út		
who mit		
why miért		
yes igen		
you te		

Read and write the sentence!

Read	Trace	Write
away el		
baby baba		
back vissza		
ball labda		
bear medve		
been volt		

Read and write the sentence!

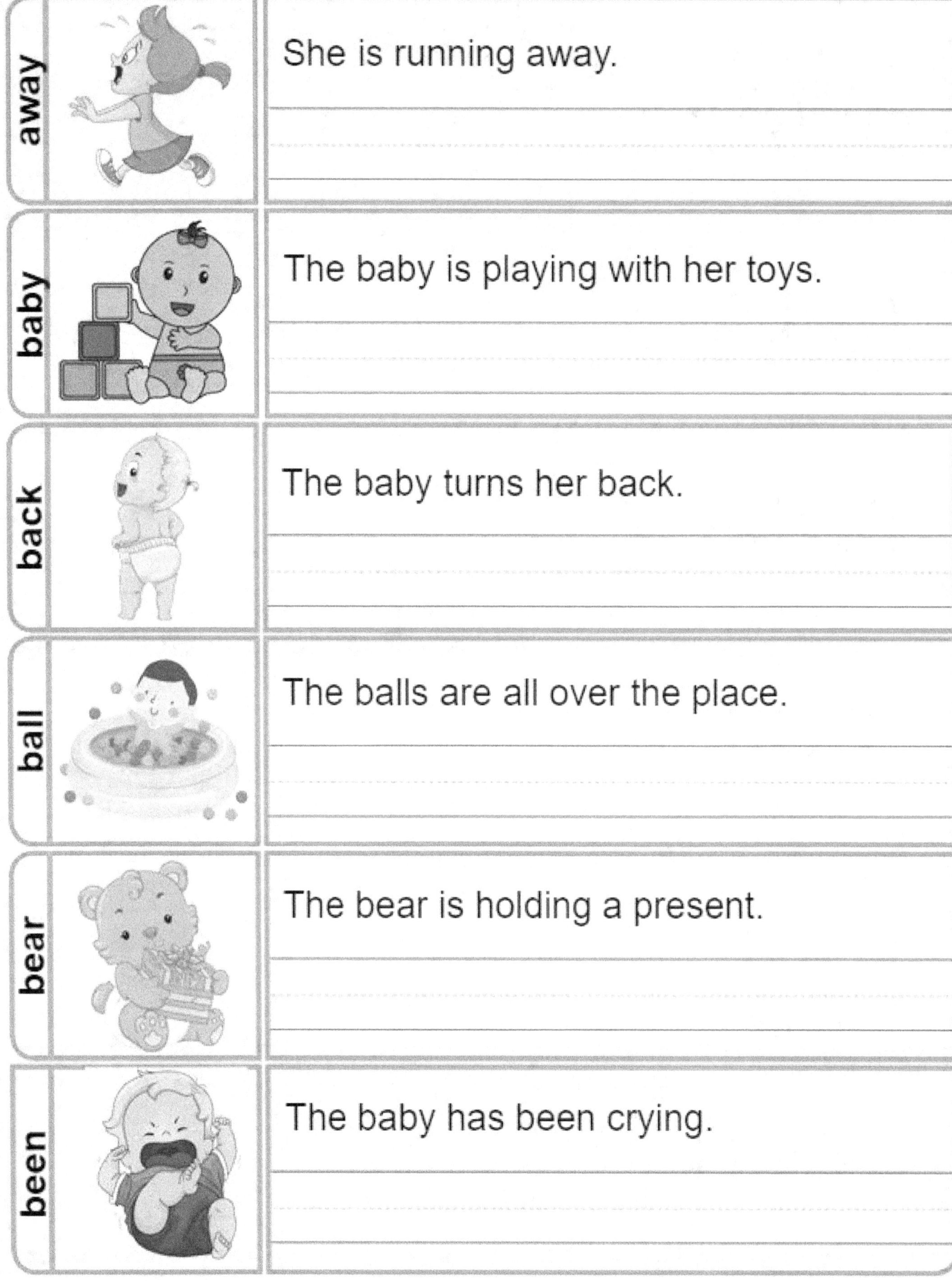

away		She is running away.
baby		The baby is playing with her toys.
back		The baby turns her back.
ball		The balls are all over the place.
bear		The bear is holding a present.
been		The baby has been crying.

Read	Trace	Write
bell harang		
best legjobb		
bird madár		
blue kék		
boat hajó		
both mindkét		

Read and write the sentence!

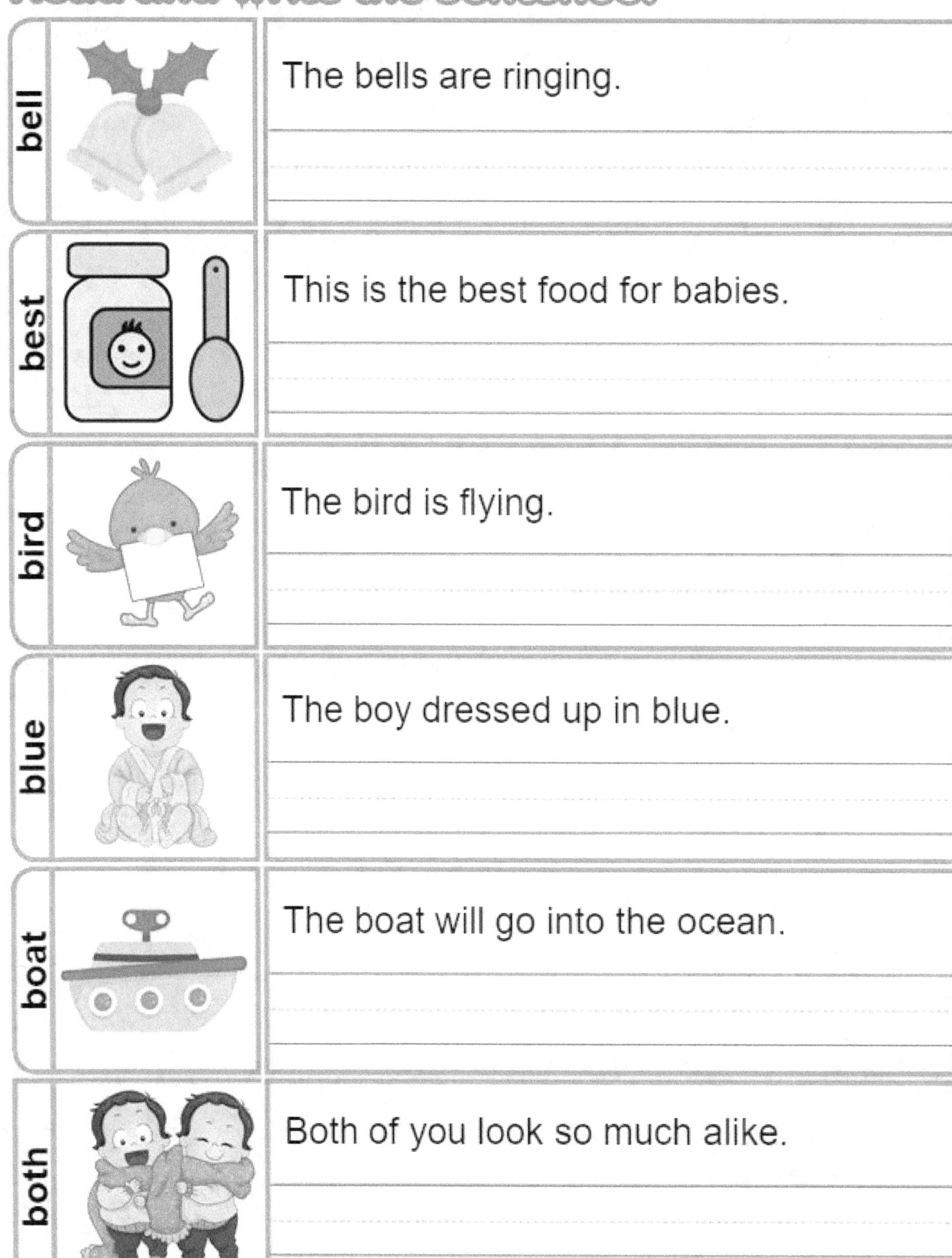

bell — The bells are ringing.

best — This is the best food for babies.

bird — The bird is flying.

blue — The boy dressed up in blue.

boat — The boat will go into the ocean.

both — Both of you look so much alike.

Read	Trace	Write
cake torta		
call hívás		
came jött		
coat kabát		
cold hideg		
come jön		

Read and write the sentence!

cake		The cake is for your birthday.
call		She is calling for somebody.
came		She came with her bag.
coat		The girl is wearing her coat.
cold		The baby feels cold.
come		Come here to the slide!

Read	Trace	Write
corn kukorica		
does csinál		
doll baba		
done kész		
door ajtó		
down le-		

Read and write the sentence!

corn	The corn tastes good.
does	Does that thing taste bad?
doll	She is hugging her doll.
done	I've done reading my book.
door	They open the door.
down	The boy turns his head down.

Read
Trace
Write
draw
húz
duck
kacsa
fall
esik
farm
tanya
fast
gyors
feet
láb

Read and write the sentence!

Read	Trace	Write
find megtalálja		
fire tűz		
fish hal		
five öt		
four négy		
from tól től		

Read and write the sentence!

find	They are finding something.
fire	The fire is blazing and dangerous.
fish	The fish are swimming in the ocean.
five	You get birthday gifts for turning five.
four	The lion is turning four today.
from	She will draw a picture of her flower.

Read	Trace	Write

full

His backpack is full of things.

game

This game is enjoyable.

gave

She gave something to her friend.

girl

The girl is sad because of something.

give

The baby gives her mommy something.

goes

She goes to the forest.

Read
Trace
Write
good
jó
grow
nő
hand
kéz
have
van
head
fej
help
segítség

Read and write the sentence!

good	The baby is acting very well today.
grow	My plant will grow!
hand	My hand is touching the wall.
have	She will have lots of friends.
head	My head is round.
help	They help each other wash the clothes.

Read
Trace
Write
here
itt
hill
hegy
hold
tart
home
itthon
hurt
sért
into
#NAME?
ugrás

Read and write the sentence!

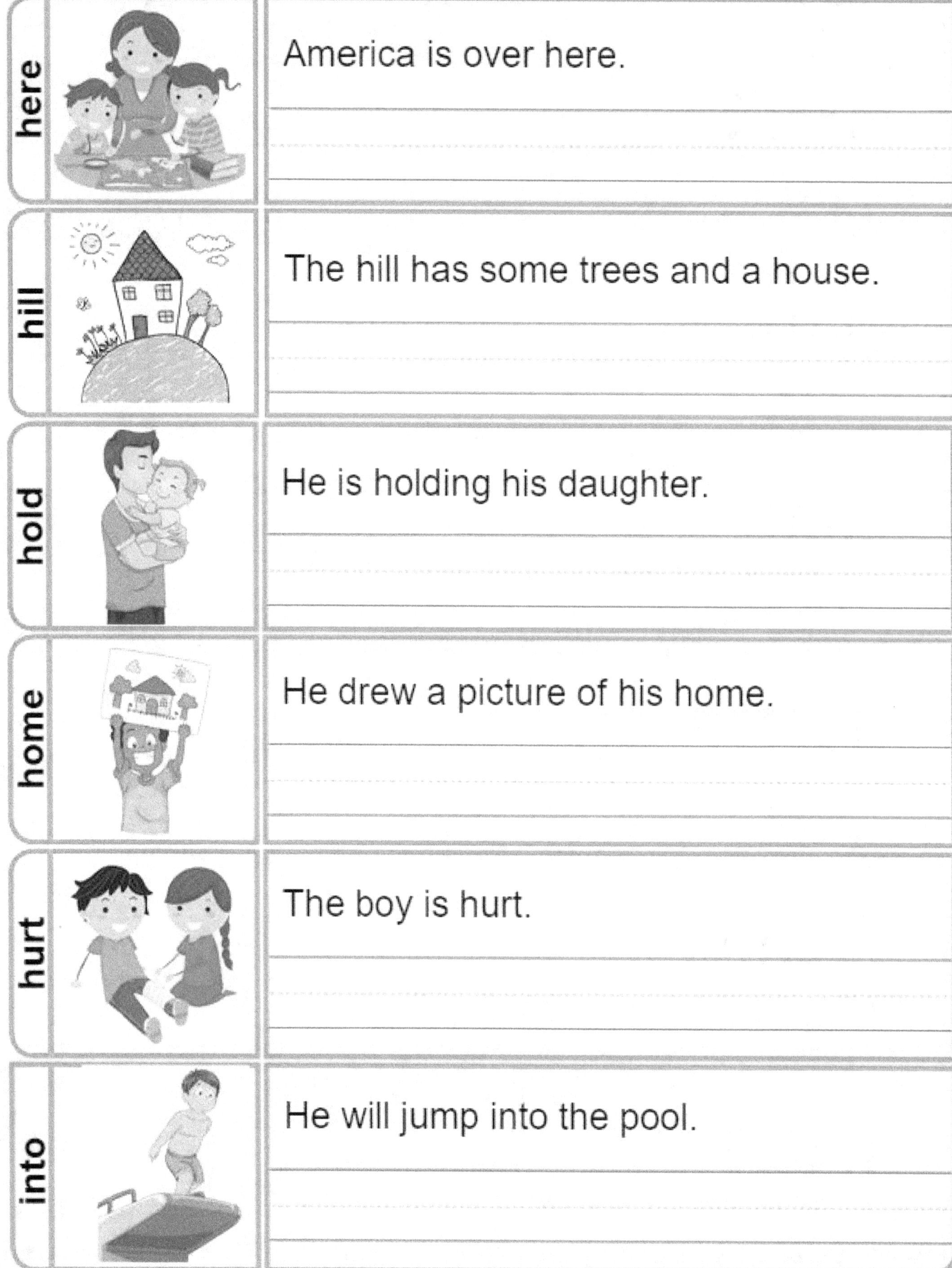

Read
Trace
Write
jump
éppen
just
tart
keep
kedves
kind
tudni
know
mint
like
élő

Read and write the sentence!

jump	The cat jumped on the cushion.
just	The arrival of the plane just arrived.
keep	She keeps thinking about it.
kind	The woman is kind to the girl.
know	They know that they will go over there.
like	He likes to ride on the horse.

Read	Trace	Write
live hosszú		
long néz		
look készült		
made készült		
make sok		
many tej		

live		They all live together.
long		The pencil is very long.
look		They are looking at something.
made		They made a promise.
make		They are going to make something.
many		He has many shirts.

Read	Trace	Write
milk sokkal		
much kell		
must név		
name fészek		
nest egyszer		
once csupán		

Read and write the sentence!

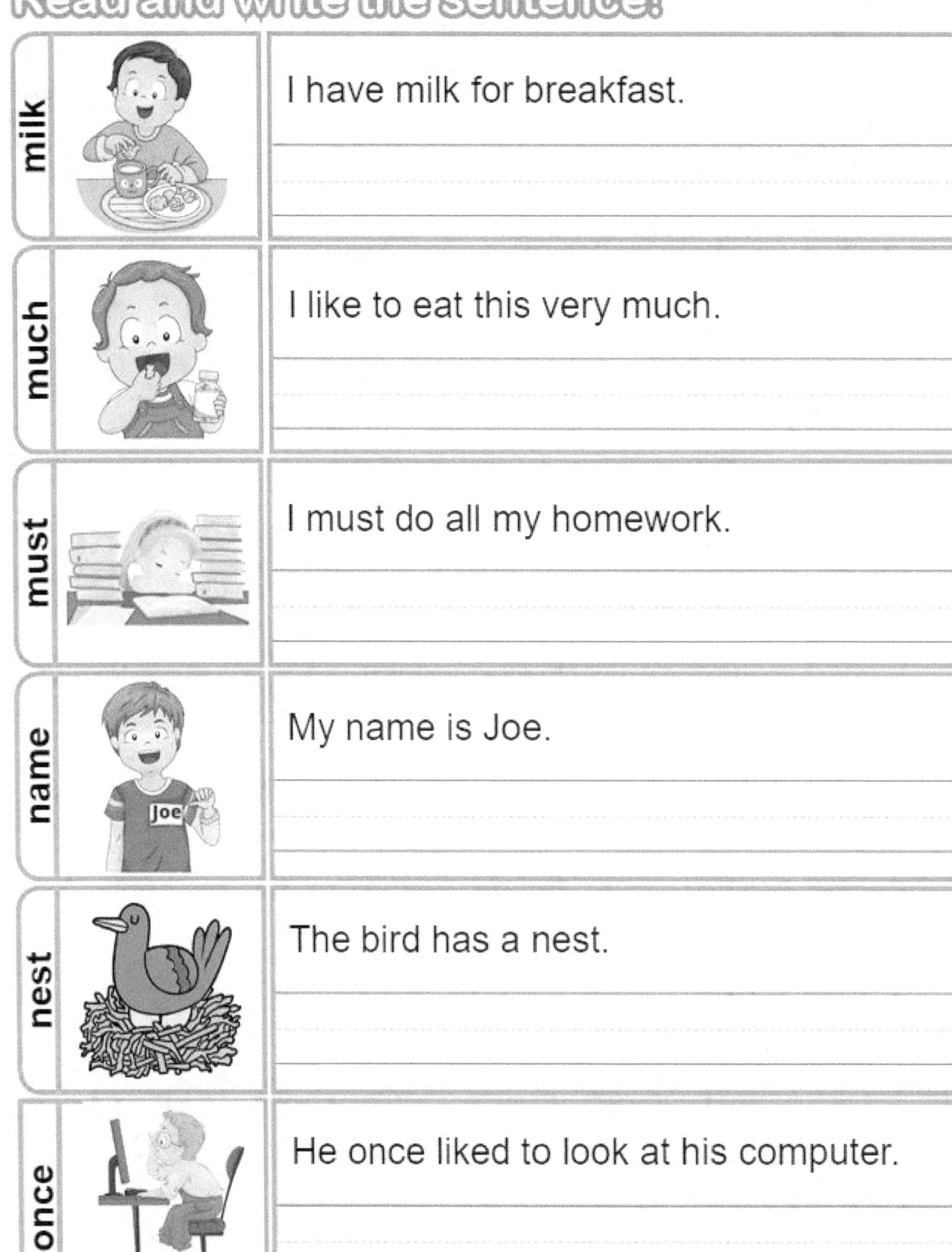

Read
Trace
Write
only
nyisd ki
open
felett
over
szed
pick
játék
play
húzni
pull
eső

Read and write the sentence!

only	There is only one student.
open	He wants to open the door.
over	The class is over.
pick	She picked up something.
play	They like to play together.
pull	She is pulling on her friend's hair.

Read
Trace
Write
rain
olvas
read
lovagol
ride
gyűrű
ring
mondott
said
mag
seed
cipő

Read and write the sentence!

rain		The rain is not going to hit us.
read		She likes to read books.
ride		The baby is riding on a toy horse.
ring		The bird is holding a ring in its beak.
said		She said hello to her neighbor.
seed		The seeds are going to plant.

Read
Trace
Write

shoe
előadás

show
énekel

sing
hó

snow
néhány

some
dal

song
hamar

Word	Sentence
shoe	Her shoes are cute and purple.
show	This map shows the location.
sing	The baby can sing along.
snow	I like to play snow.
some	These are some of my toys.
song	I will sing a song in the talent show.

Read	Trace	Write
soon állj meg		
stop vesz		
take mond		
tell hogy		
that őket		
them akkor		

Read and write the sentence!

soon	The eggs will hatch soon.
stop	The teacher says to stop.
take	They take some flowers.
tell	She is telling a story.
that	That bird dressed up as Santa.
them	He likes to eat them.

Read	Trace	Write
then ők		
they ez		
this idő		
time fa		
tree esetén		
upon nagyon		

Read and write the sentence!

then	Then, I will go to bed.
they	They are running to school.
this	This is my duck.
time	The time always moves on.
tree	There are lots of green trees in the park.
upon	Once upon a time, there was a princess.

Read	Trace	Write
very séta		
walk akar		
want meleg		
warm mosás		
wash jól		
well ment		

very	The baby is lovely.
walk	They are walking on the sidewalk.
want	The baby wants more milk.
warm	The bath is warm.
wash	She is going to wash the dishes.
well	He can save money well.

Read	Trace	Write
went vannak		
were mit		
what mikor		
when akarat		
will szél		
wind szeretnék		

Read and write the sentence!

went	The crocodile went to the pond.
were	There were lots of toys.
what	What is the lion doing?
when	When are you going to wake up?
will	Will I get it in?
wind	The wind is blowing fiercely.

Read	Trace	Write
wish val vel		
with faipari		
wood munka		
work a ti		
your ról ről		
about utána		

Read and write the sentence!

wish		I wish you a happy Christmas!
with		He is with his sister.
wood		He is stacking up wooden blocks.
work		He is going to work in his tractor.
your		Your baby is wearing a yellow suit.
about		It's about to be 12:30.

Read	Trace	Write
after újra		
again alma		
apple fekete		
black kenyér		
bread hoz		
bring barna		

Read and write the sentence!

after		The teacher calmed them after they fought.
again		He did it again!
apple		The apple is red and juicy.
black		The crow is black.
bread		My breakfast is bread and jam.
bring		He is bringing his project.

Read	Trace	Write
brown visz		
carry szék		
chair tiszta		
clean tudott		
could nem		
don't ital		

Read and write the sentence!

Read	Trace	Write
drink nyolc		
eight minden		
every első		
first padló		
floor megtalált		
found vicces		

drink — The baby likes to drink water.

eight — You get eight gifts for turning eight!

every — Every book is colorful.

first — We won first place.

floor — She is sitting on the floor.

found — It found a hat in the streets.

Read	Trace	Write

Read and write the sentence!

funny	The rabbit thinks the joke is funny.
going	The bear is going to eat all the honey.
grass	The goat eats grass on the hill.
green	The turtle that is walking is green.
horse	The horse is magical.
house	They lived in that house.

Read	Trace	Write
kitty nevetés		
laugh könnyű		
light pénz		
money soha		
never éjszaka		
night papír		

Read and write the sentence!

kitty		The kitties are charming.
laugh		They are laughing while playing.
light		The boy will turn on the lights.
money		I have earned a lot of money.
never		The bear never ate ice cream before.
night		I will sleep on my blanket at night.

Read	Trace	Write

paper	I will draw on the paper for a project.
party	The party will be for her birthday.
right	They say we have to go right.
round	The frogs' eyes are round.
seven	The monkey can count to seven.
shall	Shall I make a garden?

Read
Trace
Write

sheep
alvás

sleep
kicsi

small
rajt

start
pálca

stick
asztal

table
köszönet

Read and write the sentence!

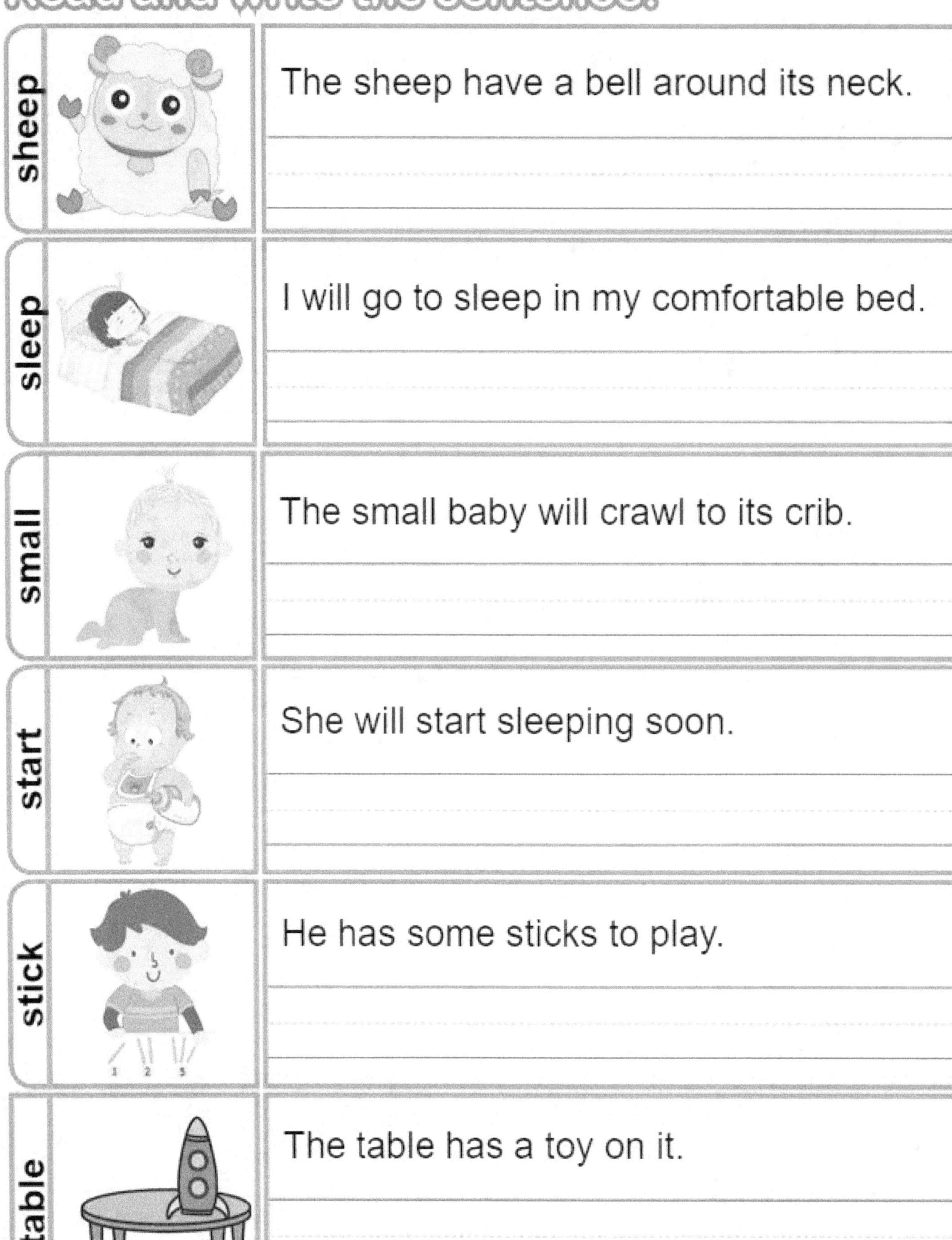

sheep	The sheep have a bell around its neck.
sleep	I will go to sleep in my comfortable bed.
small	The small baby will crawl to its crib.
start	She will start sleeping soon.
stick	He has some sticks to play.
table	The table has a toy on it.

Read
Trace
Write

thank
azok

their
ott

there
ezek

these
dolog

thing
gondol

think
azok

thank

He made a Thank you card for you.

their

They will enjoy their picnic.

there

There is something in front of you.

these

These are my eating material.

thing

The thing is broken.

think

She thinks about what she is going to draw.

Read
Trace
Write
those
három
three
ma
today
alatt
under
néz
watch
víz
water
ahol

Read and write the sentence!

those	Those are mine.
three	She will turn three today.
today	Today is a beautiful day.
under	The puppy sleeps under the blanket.
watch	They both watch the video.
water	He is drinking water after a long soccer game.

Read
Trace
Write
where
melyik
which
fehér
white
vajon
would
ír
write
mindig
always
körül

Read and write the sentence!

where	Where are we?
which	The clothes which are my sisters are colorful.
white	The sheep have white wool.
would	He would tell them a story.
write	I like to write lots of stories.
always	I am always happy that it is Christmas.

Read	Trace	Write
around előtt		
before jobb		
better gazda		
farmer apa		
father virág		
flower kert		

around — I will shuffle the shapes around.

before — Before I go to school, I kiss my mom.

better — I can make it better.

farmer — The farmer takes care of the animals.

father — My father is wearing a blue shirt.

flower — She will play with the flowers.

Read	Trace	Write
garden talaj		
ground betűk		
letter kis		
little anya		
mother magamat		
myself kérem		

Read and write the sentence!

garden	Her garden is vast and healthy.
ground	I am playing with my dog on the ground.
letter	These are the letters A, B, and C.
little	The world is small.
mother	My mother is very nice.
myself	I made these by myself.

Read	Trace	Write
please szép		
pretty nyúl		
rabbit iskola		
school lánytestvér		
sister utca		
street ablak		

Read and write the sentence!

please	Please stop pulling my hair.
pretty	She made the cake very pretty.
rabbit	The rabbit is white and soft.
school	This is the school.
sister	My sister is wearing a pink dress.
street	They are walking across the street.

Read	Trace	Write
window sárga		
yellow mivel		
because fiú testvér		
brother csirke		
chicken viszontlátásra		
goodbye reggel		

Read and write the sentence!

window		The window is open.
yellow		The ducky is yellow.
because		She will sleep because it is night.
brother		His brother is playing with him.
chicken		The chicken has hatched out of the egg.
goodbye		The animal is saying goodbye.

Read	Trace	Write
morning kép		
picture születésnap		
birthday gyermekek		
children mókus		
squirrel együtt		
together		

Read and write the sentence!

morning		He likes to ride his bike in the morning.
picture		He will take a picture.
birthday		Today is my birthday!
children		The children are doing something.
squirrel		The squirrel is cute.
together		They are sharing a bed together.